# THE GENERAL IS ASKED HIS OPINION

and other
sad songs
2002–2005
by
Omar Shapli

Not For Resale
THIS IS A FREE BOOK
www.bookthing.org
THE BOOK THING OF BALTIMORE, INC.

# The General Is Asked His Opinion and other sad songs
# 2002–2005

## Poems by Omar Shapli

twentythreebooks
Baltimore   2006

Copyright © 2006 Omar Shapli

ISBN 10: 0-9789406-0-1
ISBN 13: 978-0-9789406-0-7

Library of Congress Control Number: 2006908357

All rights reserved under International and Pan-American copyright conventions. No part of this book may be reproduced, stored in a retrieval system, or transmitted in any form, electronic, mechanical, or other means, now known or hereafter invented, without the written permission of the author.

Manufactured in the United States of America

*Cover design: Andrew Murphy*

*Website design: Elizabeth Castelletti*

Published by:

twentythreebooks
Baltimore, Maryland

www.twentythreebooks.com

## Acknowledgements

Some of these poems first appeared in a chapbook, *The General Is Asked His Opinion and other sad songs 2002–2005*, published by Pudding House Publications, 2006.

for Tryntje

*the single set of eyes*

Contents

Acknowledgements
Preface    11

Alone Among the Whippoorwills    15
Persistent Traveller    16
Another Bush    18
Constable Betrayed    19
The General Is Asked His Opinion    21
Veterans' Day    22
Barrier    23
Child's Play    24
2003    28
Ultimatum    29
Iraqi Freedom: 3 Bagatelles    30
Gabriel in a Fury    31
Agony of an Oracle    32
Tillinghast Baffled    36
Class of '48    37
Apostle    39
A Wad of Butter at Molly's    40
Return to an Old Haunt    41
Now Michael    42
People On the Beach When the Low Fog Lingers    43
Old Bolshy    44
Breakfast with W    46
Inauguration March: January 2005    47
Aix    49
Old Baathist    50
Song for Saint Cecilia    52
Theodora's Shroud    53
Weddingsong in Hard Times    54
Peterson's Song    56
Zeus's Showersong    58
Out in Early April    59

Humid Afternoon    61
Isaac's Arioso    62
Mowing    63
Brouha at the Checkpoint    64
Jitterditty in Ab    66
Friendly's on Route 2    67
A Tooth Slated for Extraction Next Wednesday    68
Audubon Sanctuary, Wellfleet    69

★ ★ ★ ★

# Screaming Owl
*a preface*

A number of these poems were initially sketched on tables at Murphy's and Molly's in Hanover, New Hampshire: evening refuges during a teaching stint at Dartmouth. The fact that my curriculum there was nothing literary or "academic" but hands-on, thumpabout *acting* may have had a bearing. The probing of text for image and character, improvising poetry without preparation but with an assumption that the complete poem already exists—all pertinent to that purpose and God help us pertinent too to the TV at the end of the bar (clearly visible but silenced by the steady uproar), puffing out surreal ghosts of a pending, then current, invasion of Iraq.

What does poetry do at such a time? Auden told us it makes nothing happen, and history won't bicker: Athenian juries gave the prize to Euripides, then went merrily off to visit the fate of Troy and its women upon towns far closer to home. The hapless soldier's sigh (if Blake had it right) ran in blood down palace walls, but was anyone looking? As for me, I order another beer and slip into the skin of folk who observe the burgeoning monster from angles that turn everything on its head.

Poetry is a messy business that demands precision. It can founder in an instant, but caulking the leaks can proliferate the messiness. Sometimes a leak needs to expand, become a grotto, draw the impulse into space utterly unexpected: a coaxing *on this side betrayal* of mystery into language. (Betrayal means fake form, or formlessness. Danger! As we used to say in Second City, when the owl screams, the hunter pisses on his foot.)

These poems were sparked by events, and also by sights and sensations that could well have been there without them. But even these—however private, however immutable—take a certain tint from transient doings that happen outside the window. Can't be helped. "Inner" moments have political consequence; politics germinates from individual insight. If political belief colors some of what follows, so perhaps does the uncertain tangle of human need and choice. The man who's coming to kill me has a point. For him it may distill to simple catharsis, but it flies like a barb out of a cloudbank—a far wider range of instinct, perception, experience. Ditto for the pundit who, with full awareness of the horror of war, finds honest cause to support it nonetheless. Politics balks, sputters, misfires destructively at such complications. Poetry thrives on them.

Complexity, of course, is an aspect of that "truth" to which we used to be told "poetry" had no access, and there are ample enough risks in wallowing in it. There are, after all, very simple, very concrete woes about which something can and must be said and done. At such moments the poet is permitted the incomparable and most joyful privilege of sounding a trumpet. Yes! Commits betrayal only by buying the possibility that virtuous action is the grave of paradox. Or (on the other foot) that paradox itself is a dead end: there's always more. And surely it doesn't take an actor to cope with complexity via various visiting personae, nor does the matter itself need to be catastrophic. Browning had ample fun that way, and Burns and Yeats and many others. For me it's social. "Tillinghast" first introduced himself in the early 70s, "McGinley" and "Peterson" a bit later. They seem to be friends, or at least familiars. And then there are the others: the onetime visitors whose orbits are far too elongated to bring them back into view this lifetime. Several may be found in this little volume. One's an angel.

None of this would have happened without the encouragement and patience of my wife, Tryntje, to whom this volume is perforce dedicated. Others who must accept their share of the blame are Arlene Bouras (for excellent advice on proofreading and perseverance), Jennifer Bosveld of Pudding House Publications (who first took positive note of many of these poems and published them as a chapbook), Clarinda Harriss of BrickHouse Books for her positive vibes and encouragement, my old friend and high school classmate Thomas J. Garbaty (prof. em., University of Michigan) for many years of warm and unflagging support, and—the ultimate culprit—Douglas William Mowbray, who undertook to publish this volume against all laws of commonsense and sagacity. My thanks to them all.

Omar Shapli
Williamstown, Massachusetts

# The General Is Asked His Opinion and other sad songs 2002–2005

## Alone Among the Whippoorwills

Think fast. Hold the
megaphone where it
shimmies least: no
foothold among the
dewy decibels! Raise
the angle and stay put.
Brace for jolts: they
are information. Be
pained by wrongsize
socks. Wheez. Doze.
Dish out the consequence.

## Persistent Traveller

tillinghast
couldn't
tell if
the post he
passed
was the
verysame
he
thought he'd
seen that
faroff day when
early snow
suffused the
glow and
cardboard
casings lit
tered the
lakebeds
and if it
was
does it
have to
mean its
all been
loops and
circles from
there to here
and headway's a
scam like
mapleflavored
beer or be
nign pet
roleum or
webaccess

with no fee

or is each
footfall
coactive with
now to hold
the past
back
where we
always needed
it to be

he
seemed to re
call two
wormholes just
below the up
per sliceoff and
nota bene here
there's only
one
so he's
finally fain to
focus brain
on tasks
at closer
range

like sift
ing with des
perate dili
gence what
ever
might be
left of the
change

## Another Bush

and what they told me was this

the visionthing eschewed by dad
lurks now in the nascent galahad

## Constable Betrayed

*more ado and a howl from the loo*

rackety tack
rackety tack
dogberry got where he couldn't get back
moon hadn't risen
house wasn't hizzen
night was a warren and prim as a prison

o where were the whispers of reticent wainmen
the elegant murmurs the scent of cacao
shunted through clumps of disconsolate trainmen
the haulers of presence the caddies of now

holy smoke
holy smoke
no one here who can get the joke
little to be
not much to see:
just the mottled meterman waiting for his fee

they that touch pitch will be surely defiled
those who dunk onions will tangle their beards
the canapé-shuckers ought not to have riled the
three little maids who turned out to be weirds

where it's at
jehosophat
wiggled and sniggled and suddenly sat
couldn't judge
would not fudge
rose to full effulgency but failed to budge

drifting to decency scarcely an option
glittering glyphs deliquesce to a scrawl
creeds and affinities up for adoption

self a simulacrum defiance a brawl while
back at the dorm
clamped to the norm
they set their silly shibboleths in cuneiform

do watermen swim home again
when minnows climb ashore
must whippersnappers snap the bat
before they deign to roar

is evil still exotic when it
simmers on the stove
and why do dingbats dawdle
in the eucalyptus grove

dogberry diddled with the lid of his chapeau
moonlight wasn't wearing well
wonking wouldn't stop
time's a rusted shackle when it interdicts the toe and
with a flash the dome will crash before those doggies hop

klippety klop
klippety klop
no place here for an
honest cop

## The General Is Asked His Opinion

A good idea? That
question has no meaning
for me. Good for what?
Isn't that Policy? Wouldn't
that be *your* menu? Oh
yes ample stew for the
pot, if that observation
assists you: flesh to the
shredder—much of ours,
more of *theirs*—but that's
our *slot* is it not: grind
the bones to prop a Policy?
Not my job to tell you it
makes sense. Mine's a
profession that makes
sense only when nothing
else does and that Sir is
*your* call. When sense
fails, tap my shoulder.
And don't think for an
instant I miss the rolling
nudge around the table,
the condescension, the
snide asides.

I only request—no, *beg* (not
easy for me)—that you track
me a trinket that can damwell
dent my palm: not a frail
daydream of clean solutions
where nothing clean abides.

## Veterans' Day

*sotto voce*

Truly my war held no great risk
to me, a divisionlevel oddjobber
on the hither fringe of the Punchbowl.
But may I not retain a certain very
humble pride in silence? Be one with
the ones who shake head sadly and stare
at the happyhour niblets as someone
further down the bar regales with
tales of bloodsoaked trails through
snowblocked passes? True I have
precious little to be silent *about*:
flashes and rumbles just over the
ridge and of course the constant
chance of tipping my tintinnabulous
Dodgethreequarter over the lip of a
tentative roadway into the deepchilled
Pukhan—oh not a lot when set beside
the great bugout and the true horrors
of nightly patrol just a few miles to
my north. What I did see more than
once was the flatout stare which told
me this guy and I had nothing to talk
about: he'd been just hours ago in a place
as remote from me as some Venusian
fulmination smashing through wreckage
that once was a cliff under perpetual
cloudcover. Tonight at this bar I vaunt
my silence in merest tribute to his.

## Barrier

when I was a lockeyed nine or ten and utterly
innocent of rabelais I marvelled at a circus
gorilla named gargantua he was big and he was
dark and when he curled his nostrils it was
hard not to hang onto the edge of the bench and I
finally put it to my mother reluctant as always to
put anything to my mother why does he not
splinter those bars with a sweep of his thumb
and wander off through the nickelaride subway
to pelham bay park for a picnic and a soda

well maybe she said just maybe he thinks it's
*we* who are locked away all safe and sound and it's
his great good fortune that we have yet to
crack the myth and be upon him

## Child's Play

*the monkey thought it all in fun*

wasn't good
where it was
though it stood
flanked by laws

epiderm
almost tame
bolted firm
to the frame

tethered well
through the heart
as the shell
flew apart

and we rose
toward the flame
that we chose
to rename

not a spark
to illume
but the dark
flash of doom

dump the fern
for the rose
take a turn
on the toes

and a whirl
in the brain
that a churl
might disdain

since the case
for reprieve
had no place
up the sleeve

of the haunt
on the hill
where the gaunt
graces still

sip their gin
with restraint
as they win
what we mayn't

should there be
more than that
when the bee
bites the cat

or the sun
fries the flesh
of the one
in the mesh

does the pain
of that fall
wipe the stain
from us all

or are roots
tougher still
than the boots
on the hill

climbing yet
to deploy
what they yet
to destroy

with the spikes
on their toes
and the pikes
up the nose

of the el
egant sheep
who must sell
what they reap

yet the spring
bubbles still
from the wing
of the hill

where the weeds
waggle hard
and the seeds
keep their guard

should a race
that wrought cause
in a place
flanked by laws

as they fought
to reclaim
what they sought
to rename

but won't see
where it's at
when the bee
bites the cat

not do well
to reflect
on the smell
of neglect

on the wham
and the bang
when the lamb
takes the fang

and return
to the whiff
of the fern
on the cliff

where the wind
traps the sand
to rescind
what was planned

and the might
y are shown
what they might
well have known

that a meek
leaf betrays
a whole week
of mondays

(should the scent
fail to please
wedge your vent
through the trees)

## 2003

*the rapture*

Deathgod presides over the Final Daze.
Dickory dock clicks the clock. Bethlehem's
where it always was and twice will not
suffice. Holywater sizzles the spout:
passionate intensity brooks no doubt.

## Ultimatum

We said You Must and They Did.
But why should mere compliance
wreck a perfectly good hunt when
tire lies heavy on tarmac? No
point to a kill if it's only done for
cause. Not our *response* they must
fear but our *whim*: we will be like
the Turkish sultan whose privilege
it was to snuggle with his
arquebus behind the seraglio's
lofty crenelations and pop off
ten random passersby per day.
Hey! And who's to say it won't
be for the best? Even random
destruction destroys *some* things
we might best do without: it's only
apology and weakness of appetite
prompts the backfire. Yes, best they
should fear us not for *their* choice
but for *ours*. There'll never again be a
swath of turf where our sweet lads can't
wander at will. And the speedbumps,
the ones who willfully miss the point?
Let them die in their dustbaked batches.
No sheen of martyrdom to elevate
their absence: just the blurred-out
shroud of axiomatic irrelevance.

And doesn't the food get better
war by war?

## Iraqi Freedom: 3 Bagatelles

*Enemy Dead*

Soldiers. Fair game by the helpless thousands.
Endless acres of decay: the laziest way
to formulate an argument. Bury them fast.

*A Flyer Who Likes to Be Called
    Captain Killerchick*

Partytime jollity and centuries of sexual
rage cling to the soubriquet. What
better shelter for a corpsemaker than
to find it an overdue occupation?

*A Biblebred GI Writes Home*

The problem is not that they are
not like us but that they are
like us far beyond our reckoning.

Righteousness is a blight upon the soil
and God has twenty tongues too many.

## Gabriel in a Fury

*tuba mirum spargens sonum*

I told him the way to the stars lies
through the heart of the earth and
today I find him digging a hole.
Damnation! Words are not The
Word! To bind a truth to the crude
tools which release it is sacrilege.

## Agony of an Oracle

*tough times at The Times*

War: I buy it. Sweated out
the thought: bought it whole.

Was *there* for my leaders who
let me down *loutishly*. Baffled
by Why they befouled the What.
And when isness impends (well
mirrored in the eyes of friends!)
to stipple *me* as liar or as fool…
Oh piddle. Piddle riddle and rot.
*Why* must that aloe tumble from
its pot like a languid Niagra?

It's not that the tick hadn't
grappled my scalp from the
start: never did doubt the
truly massivist mucro was
that magma of kids whose
hate tickles more than the
pesky thump in the ribcage.
Oh I knew and I lucidly
bruited that the screaming
deadmen who blasted the
towers were's fully primed
for secular Saddam as ever
they were for *us*! Didn't
we share a certain smug
targetude? Would even he
or even *we* take a clout more
exasperatingly irksome
than the prim rebuke of a
Swedish professor with glasses?
Yes I knew or I guessed that the
mechanisms were long gone,

trashed when trashing was the
hotminted mandate. Yet I did
believe that *doing* the bullyboy
might clear the way for a kind
of tectonics not consonant with
helterskelter vivicide. And
there's the matter of *them*,
the Ramallah rumblers who
are their own switchblades:
might *they* have simmered to
quiescence when their survivors—
dust having cleared from their
bulldozed houses—could
expect no more munificence
from the bosom of the Baath?
Is that the way the heart works?
Is it not perhaps reasonable? Is
*reason* reasonable? And why
can't that wobbly passionflower
retain its dadblasted water?

In any case it was never
supposed to go on this long.
Condi told us the first week's
snipers were like the Wehrwolfs
of '45, but did lone Americans
really fear to mosey through
München by '47? Doesn't scan,
doesn't scan: goodhearted
occupations bear small
semblance one to tuther
and even the harshest
lessons of the 30s can be
read both ways. Yet the
outcome, and I am absolutely
certain of this—the swat, the
crunch, the crumble of ghastly
statuary—was as right as

anything can be that depends
for its effect upon mutilative
slaughter of thousands of
actual functioning bipeds.

Might there have been a
better way? That question
freezes all motion, stops
choice in its tracks, sends
waves of terrified GIs back
to their ships in the choppy
waters off a tomb called
Omaha. Action's incumbent
upon us. There must be Cause.
Not religion please, though like
electroplated crusaders we do
have our old man of the mountain
squinting at our doings through
cracks in the crags. He and we
have come to share that ancient
dingaling: only in one way can
we mean what we say and that
way's the ripping of flesh and
bone. Small matter whose.
Certainly not our own: no,
we've both found the trick
of selling to *others* the
finer delights of selfdemise:
either dulce et decorum or the
Prophet's paradise.

Consider well that potted orangetree:
thirst its only ticket from absurdity.

Iraqis themselves? They are kindling
for the counterburn twixt us and those who
wish us blended into solar wind. Unfair,
sure, and iffy in extremis, but might not that

injustice find a balance among other things
that stir within the offal? Can't the cradle
that produced *us* give *itself* a better whiff of
things asimmer in the ancient cellars? Oh
have a care with those two patient rivers!
Consider the hard birth that happened
between them, the thing that found its
shape, that grew, that flourished on those
banks. May Hammurabi yet invoke law
over random chaos as sunlight pokes its
way to metal through rolling billows of
pulverized obsidian? Would that be hope?
Or censure too tremendous to be softened in
a third caustic cup of sizzling Sumatran?

There's Indja to extrapolate and China to expound.
And a storebought orchid's neither lost nor found.

## Tillinghast Baffled

tilling
hast could
not
recall just
whom it was
who
held his
shape
for one out
of focus inst
ant then let it
poof
into forget
fulness: there
being no
subst
ance to the
matter and no
energy neither
twould seem the
thought could
leave no
ripple
so where thinks
tillinghast
does
HE come in

## Class of '48

'42 and billy loves sal
they long to diddle and maybe they shall
the dead drift back from guadalcanal
*when do i slip from this skin*

mathematics and walter scott
green gymlockers and bigtoe rot
ration stamps in gaping pot
*when do i slip from this skin*

we'll buy 'em a jeep in '43
paste the stickers for miniscule fee
there'll be no rides for such as we
*when do i slip from this skin*

wednesday assembly on the edge
honorguard and godless pledge
titania tangled in the hedge
*when do i slip from this skin*

victory bikes in '44
wounded hearts behind the door
awash in wishes to weep no more
*when do i slip from this skin*

'45 lights up the sky
could be we won't have to die
isotopes get in the eye
*when do i slip from this skin*

'46 and pick up sticks
nothing so soiled that we can't fix
primed to the gills we get in our licks
*when do i slip from this skin*

drop a hem in '47
regents guard the gate to heaven
zion castigates ernest bevin
*when do i slip from this skin*

thumping about in roseate haze
testing our toes to the end of days
new studebaker goes both ways
*when do i slip from this skin*

'48 and a prague-ish chill
jan masaryk goes over the sill
jitter and skitter and pop a pill
*when do i slip from this skin*

warbirds rustle and start to fly
chiggers abrade the astonished eye
could be we'll all have to die
*when do i slip from this skin*

where to piddle and where to hide
gird your loins the principal cried
baffled to blazes we certainly tried
*when do i slip from this skin*

## Apostle

a mere quarter century back when i
was about to be out of a job and none
of the people who'd been telling me for
years to let them know if ever i found
myself free to pick up stakes and come
play with them seemed able to answer
a thought a letter or even a phonecall
it was old sills who told me not to
lose heart because the way society
is now constituted it's physically
impossible to slip backward out of the
middle class no matter how dismal
the view down the ill-lit sidestreet
and oh golly how desperate i must
have been to grasp at that thought
with the same sense of relief
that bouyed the historybattered
athenians when another paul gave
them a whiff of the unknown god

## A Wad of Butter at Molly's

The right and foresides spell form:
humanescent twiddles suggesting
some sort of lowgrown vegetation.
Left and rear it's all over: graded
but not even flat, formless to my
conditioned eye, pure devastation.
My knife did this: call the troops
home.

## Return to an Old Haunt

Yes, this is the place, less Frank the
barkeep. He knew the good beers,
harbored the special vintage, and now
it simply fits the pattern. This is, one
might say, an abode of competence:
ability less poetry. Priced too high for
that: I'll not stay. Curious to recall how
an air of serious concern coupled with
simple precision of *modus* could foster
a notion that this was a haven I somehow
deserved. Now it's too good for me.

## Now Michael

*Mr. Moran, 2/5/04*

An ear.
A powerful round man
with a direct heart. *I hear you I see*
*you and this is what I'm ready to do.*
Swirls of devotion now frozen to a block.

Companions congregate. Shaken and
baffled they need to know
where did the high fun go:
generosity, sadness, that
ardent making of things.
Yes the bubble did struggle
but never quite burst: pushed
by year, day, hour from the strong
and busy doings back to the kernel
itself. A rare destination,
let time never touch it.

At last: a husk. Love
lived in it. Take thanks.

### People on the Beach When the Low Fog Lingers

Moving not so very much they
cling to outline but lose all hint of
physiognomy as waves lap lazy
out of haze and looking out or is it
up find not a hint of binding edge
and when at last the dizzy glare
ignites the capstone, space is
clear as wobbled sphere where
fringes wriggle in the wind and
substance shifts (rescind rescind).

## Old Bolshy

Different songs keep different throngs in line.
But may not a man be kept in different lines all
at once by some novel disposition of ideational
harmonics? The Party for a start had it wrong about
Church: old Solzhenitsyn made that perfectly plain
to plainbrain Brezhnev. Religion, army, demands
of job, fellowship—all lines for people to be kept
in. State must give them welcome. No need for
them to return the favor! They do it anyway, do
it by sipping their tea. They, within State, are order.
Order's good: gross grabberism not. Church
knows that. Party knew that. But people are weak,
easily tempted by things they'll never need. Give
them something better than their heart's desire:
give them service! Serve them well and let them
in turn serve that other thing that's bigger yet than
*they*: God, State, Populus: why quibble? The
principle's certainly at root religious, a notion
lacking in comfort to some of us old ones. Not
that comfort isn't important: one ought to ease
into political philosophy as nicely as I into this
monstrous chaise, now dilapidated but the
snazziest we could produce back then when it
and I were somewhat newer and verymuch better
to be. A new class said Djilas and maybe so. But
who *else* was up to the task? Doesn't every great
movement require a cadre? And were we not
acolytes, at our best striving to enrich the scope
of awareness, of confidence in accomplishment,
of general closeness to the Deity? Corruption?
Of course. But not what you think, you with
your tongue stuck in a cluckcluckcluck. Not
the corruption of a few extra goods, a few special
shops, the tingle of control over lives of our

neighbors: those were there all right, but where
are they not? No, ours was the corruption of
silence, of acquiescence to inefficiency, of
holding our true competence deep in check while
massive stupidities cracked the very veins of
confraternity. We tricked ourselves into being
puzzled. Yet was the problem any more massive
than, say, the devastation of the nation back in
'45? And didn't we send a clear beam through
all the reeking wreckage to marshal exhaustion,
grief, even despair itself toward the doing of a
true secular miracle? Rubble and corpses cleared,
factories reared, schools and homes and farms and
dizzying dams back where they belonged, rail and
road connecting them, all within a scant five years?
Could we do that and not cope with a few failings
of mental architecture among tired tetrarchs like
the one who now leans forward to offer you a glass
of kvass? Toodle and tut. Folk will grow tired of
Self. They will find it a phantasm, a holographic
projection of someone else's prosperity. When
the peddler becomes a shopkeeper and gobbles
enough of the other shopkeepers to become an
oligarch, then they'll see whose self is truly
served. Perhaps (this is the maddest of hopes) the
oligarchs will devour one another until there's only
one Great Oligarch! When that day comes, State
will require but a single gulp to restore socialism:
could that perhaps be what Putin's waiting for?
Then won't we *come* with a rumtumtum! One
redemptive surge to clear the clutter from
the veins and metabolize All Ambition into
Ambition for All! Ignis fatuus you say, but
quite enough glow to warm this frozen toe.
And what's a Faith without a Resurrection?

★ ★ ★ ★

## Breakfast with W

> *Moonlight Diner & Grille:*
> *Wednesday, November 5, 2004*

He accepts a slice of my
blueberry pancake and
braces his back against
the pinkwood casement.
In faroff Mesopotamia the
marines prepare to stir the
ugly gumbo: they say they
mourn the recent fallen
and they fear tomorrow
and they're pained to be
hated while being goodguys
but *semper fi* eclipses *why*.
Across my table: no doubts.
David has slain his tens of
thousands. Human misery's
but a passing flash and
four short years may
well take us to the Final
Daze: it's good it's good
it's very good, and ready
for the rapture he swipes a
mapleflavored mote from the
very edge of that evanescent grin.

# Inauguration March: January 2005

*("The Sunne doth gild our Armour..." Henry V, iv:ii)*

hello to a sun that can corrugate armor
step off with a crash to befuddle the doubtful
swing to the lilt of the rattling gadgets there's
cash to be stashed at kirkuk

steer clear of the fussbudget call to the colors
internalize target: eschew interruption:
eulogize uniforms (glad you're not filling one
when you slip off to kirkuk)

wildcat time on the sands above basrah
bomb or a bullet is grist for the gamble
pick up the beat and defray the expenses
make it or bust in kirkuk

a bang and a thump and a brassy convection
whoop and a holler and damned if you don't
toot and a boomlay for all petty bushwah
siphon the cream in kirkuk

rebuff the recruiters agleam in the morning
armies are socialist by definition
why marry the state if the state is the problem
gold in the ground at kirkuk

be one with the cowboys who know no denial
saddle up contracts and rope in the prize
deliver the consequence wrapped in white linen
coffined and coifed in kirkuk

weighted and plated and armed to the ballocks
we'll pop at gyrenes who would dampen our doings
flaunt heavy lettuce when *they* waggle duty
banging the dog in kirkuk

wassail to the chief in our spiked cocacola
nature abhors an invidious vacuum we'll
face down the haze with a farragut look
DAM THE EUPHRATES and rear condominiums
and wham the slamdunk in kirkuk

## Aix

> *Charlemagne mulleth a missive from Byzantium read to him by Einhardt just after supper.*

You tell me a man who dresses in many
colors and was never able to learn the
trick of reading his own capitularies
cannot inherit old Caesar's wreath,
but what can you know of such matters
you in your great gleaming gazebo? Is
there fresh meat in your teeth when you
sing God's praises? Do you sweat through
your silken tunics? Are you able to be
blunt? I tell you the one true trick to th'
imperium is transgression minus misgiving.
No doubts, no wavering, strike hard when
authority demands it, acknowledge no
flaw. And oh yes embrace the option of
slaughter when many least expect it. The
great beauty of a bloodspill is it always
serves a purpose: error's impossible.
Without it the web snaps to shreds.

I can write my name, or most of it, the K,
the R, L and S each bursting at the tip
of a hairline stretched nicely toward all
four points of creation. Consonants are
the bone, the thing capable of holding
other things: vowels are transient, messy,
frequently treacherous. The web's where
they live, there at the center, growing,
shrinking, shifting shape and sound,
quite indistinguishable from men like
yourselves for whom modulation is
everything. Like you they do not have
to be named. They are Civilization.
Herding them and *you* is what I'm for.

Ever pick your teeth with the
bristle of a boar?

## Old Baathist

    *(recalling Michel)*

Yes it would have been better if
the Founder had lived a little longer:
see us baffled and rattled, quite bled to
the bone and in no slight need of his
prickly advice! Did he not teach us to
pronounce the word Secular? No easy
fit for our language. Unity, progress,
be Arab, be human in a human world.
Not even the nasty little hijacker could
utterly ransack that vision. No, it took
a clutch of Americans blasting all our
markets to blazes in the name of a
pooka called The Market.

Hard to recall that eighty
years back when told we had to
have a Protector we opted for that
verysame America but much to the
relief of the brits and the frogs it
was those normalcyprone yankees
who had the sense to say no. They
had that canny cigarstore wisdom
back then. Now the best they dare
hope is that we'll find a way to be
just enough at eachother's throats to
keep out of everyone's way but not
so much as to staunch the bloody oil.
Oho. We writhe in the killingpits:
we are everybody's bullseye and my
veryown nieces, raised to raise their
heads, now find it prudent to cover
that same appendage as they assay a
whiff of the mutual air! What would
he tell us, old Aflaq, sad and patient

at his favorite table in the waning
afternoon? Be a new kind of Arab,
be human, see with clear eyes, leave
the priests and the mullahs to their
mumbles and build with your own
hands the best world your minds can
imagine. No Iraq, no Syria or Levant,
just a rolling swell of siblings ready
to raise ourselves toward a single
shared felicity. Oh let the Kurds
have their Kurdistan, the Turks
stay perched on their oversized
trowel, the Farsi continue to think
they're better than everyone else:
we require no alloy except our Arab
selves. And do tell the foreigners,
without malice, their day here's over.

Excuse me: the young corporal
seems ripe for a buy.

## Song for Saint Cecilia

*the emperor packs it in*

none commanded wider space
than did he
spain peru and mexico
slabs of italee

stretches of the bony north
at his command
spite of the jowly jake who railed
here i stand

came that day he went away
just like that
left the throne without a moan
with sandal sack and mat

the wheezy organ that he lugged
expounding paradox
bade him note what had been his
from high among the rocks

a triad teasing soul and ear
toward sad redact
daring him to see and hear
what now he lacked

and didn't the raw bellows pique
some panharmonic elf
to clear the dew and lock in view
that thing itself

and wasn't it a grand cadeau
tit for tat
to spy what there but empty air where
he had sat

## Theodora's Shroud

And there we have an eruption,
a line, almost a fence of purple
iris. Hard to imagine anything less
naturally linear. Perhaps not a line:
perhaps a cascade from highest to
least high with swirling ruffs that
raffishly nix such propriety. And
tucked within the petal-go-round:
a glassy shadow to slow the pulse.

Color of power (hence of death),
it denies light while hoarding it:
evokes blackness with a glow.
Into it in sweeping spirals drifts the
eye, shapes and edges slipping past
like old hopes that meant as little in
blossom as now they do in dry denial.
A termless universe, vast as any,
capricious enough yet perverse in
refusal to give up the notion of form.

Comfort can show itself in manners
that make no sense at all: a pang of
loss, an aspiration denied, a bank of
growling clouds suddenly blocking
the afternoon sun. Here's another.

## Weddingsong in Hard Times

*Grace and Tarik Do the Thing: 1 / 1 / 05*

What are they up to now?
What poignant contingencies replete
with powerpacked flukiness and sinewy
sourpussing can they have possibly come
up with? Roses? Bones? Starlight?
What lofty hightension and preposterous
parabolas have they taken it upon
themselves to swizzle out there in
the nattering firmament? What's the
*pattern* up there? A racecourse for
reckless rabbits taking on two wheels
the dreadfullest curve that nobody no
nobody in this greatguns toughlove
economy has managed to negotiate
except by weirdo preposturing and
holymoly selling off all that was left
of last year's streamlined crockery?
What are they *up* to?

Oh yes love. The widget that won't
quantify. A luminescence ping'd
and pong'd in dizzy repetition by
antipodal eyeballs. Curious optical
principle! Incessant reflection failing
to fade toward fuzziness.

Most strange most strange. Comparison
stuck before it starts. Doesn't rabbit make
the curve good and easy and settle safe on
a homestretch that crackles toward a whole
gleaming sheaf of new beginnings?

No. Metaphor fails the lowspeed crash
test. These two make strength in one

another, a process solid as Presence.
No place for perky persiflage! The
thing has mass and yes momentum:
divination dives for the foxholes.
And malicious necessity, out there
pawing the pathway? Let it prepare
to duck and duck fast: love takes
no prisoners.

Then what share of the air for us, the lucky
logrollers here for the niblets? Is there no
Law of the Conservation of Synergy? Let
them dicker with the gadgetry and find a way
to preserve the goodtime surge. Yes! Pack it
and save it right there in the pantry with the
extra lightbulbs.

Caulks cracks in wintertime. Lasts.

## Peterson's Song

> *The old grabber lays it out as Tillinghast
> digests a grilledcheese and stares at his pickle.*

You have to lose. No use wagging your
manicured dreadlocks: you're toast. Your
truly generous overview, your modulated
weltschmerz, undeniably accurate analyses,
prescient predictions and terrifying toxins,
your rage, even your—what shall we call it?
Love? None of these dislodge the merest
flake from the bathroom ceiling. You
cannot win, and the reason is this: your
universe empowers complexities. Mine?
Why, mine denies them utterly. *Utterly*:
alien territory for you, yes? How see both
sides *utterly*? You reject perfection to
wallow in the shifting sands, while for *me*
perfection's intrinsic to effort. Yes! No
way to fail! While *you* wriggle your way
through comprehension, alliance, intricate
balance of interests—I go for the gherkin
outright. Give it a tickle yourself: room
for all! Scuttle compunction. If everybody
sucks the heartsblood out of everybody,
everybody wins! True, the throbbing blob
may dodge, thwack back, bloody my highset
forehead: no matter. I'll slip down a notch,
but the Will still encompasses the entire
rotunda. With you, ideal and ambition take
corruption one from the other, but my road
is pure. Appetite's incorruptible.

Oh I see: you require a less parochial
perspective. Doesn't the human nebula
swirl in upon itself with incremental
momentum? Manic multiplication plus

equally pertinacious empowerment of
smaller and smaller subsets (right down
to the highschool physics dropout who for
thirty bucks and a date with his sister will
easily inveigle his exclassmate qua
automechanic into crunching together
some messy little mechanism of wholesale
biocide)—you grant that it's thinkable?
Within the realm? Add instantaneous
communication and a widespread capacity
to plant a boot on your front stoop and
what's the residue in your afternoon
latte? Sys-tem-atic resolution? Hardly.
Just snips and jiggles and consequent
wriggles. A tap here, a clack there, a
wishful whimper of unfruited philosophy.

Me? I abide by Church Triumphant: raw
salvation for the isolated soul. I hold with
World Without End: won't there always
be something to seek, seize, defend? Vaster
the cataclysm, grander the Chance. Failure's
loss of energy, of sharp and roving eye, of
appetite, of Faith. It won't happen to me:
not in this universe. When the planet itself
shivers to fragments, cast a final glance at
*me*, bobbing my way through the airless
moans and glowing boulders, eye fixed
hard on the one drifting chunk that yet
sports an unexploited flower.

## Zeus's Showersong

*cloudy morning on Olympos*

rumtumtiddle with the rantantan
better not diddle with the strawberry man
owns what he smashes with brash élan
a towel for the shower and a snap at the fan
some couldn't take it and away they ran
been like that since the world began
all who diddle with the strawberry man
find that the fire pains less than the pan
(rumtumtiddle with the rantantan)

## Out in Early April

spring catches me napping:
infiltrates exhaustion and
suddenly there it
is way up ahead well
beyond the
doublebent birch though
last fall's leaves
aren't
yet part of the
soil so corruption's
underway underfoot but

so's something else and
spring nips me high and dry
time rips and tears at
defunct trunks
with a vengeance so
death's somewhere
close:
small holes already
speckle the freshveined leaves
and the path has the presumption to
gurgle at my ankles

hello path

spring yes
excremental mud obscures
the gutters and cherish a
glimpse of tiny
ferns fragile pagodas that
utterly deny the politics of the day

puff hard puff

clear and steady: trees
swing both ways like a
massive grin with me the tongue
and here suddenly's my
stone: time to plant a foot and
tootle a prayer

omigod dandelions their time for
glory before troopers
hit the silk golden
punctuation like spurts of
sunsperm everywhichway to
asterisk this day

and here's a tree
where two birds once lectured me
on the vanity of despair i
set them to it and they
pierced me painful:
true they
did give me a
message that might
have been hope but was it
my own domestic hope or
simply something that pulls
me along in its wake

commotion cracks the margin: huge
welldigger mauls the
postcard and
there's that biker rounding
the bend: small ankledangling
children swat each other from
lower branches and
death will have to
do some catching up

downhill's tough on the toes

## Humid Afternoon

When trees turn nonporous in the heavy air
(green blocksolid, shadings a shell), when
mist congeals on distant slopes (fallow algae
noted through rifts, detail assumed yet
quite unprovable), when the slightest breeze
seems awkward at best, at worst catastrophic
(cracking rigidity, threat to all structure),
then is it not odd to spot a flower, a single
bloodred blip where it makes no sense, a
squeal of mischief flatout inappropriate to
the day and a challenge to the niceties of
molecular law?

Order's only a layer: that's reassuring.

## Isaac's Arioso

If love(you say)'s beside the point
then what engine is it *you* advance as
the pertinacious pivot? Bread? Kruption?
Oh: or eek-ohn-omics? Enthronement
of pecksniffian plutology as God's
unquestioned will on earth? Or praps I
sniff a certain raw exhaustion to balance
that vasty barrenness, the universe itself!
You'd set love aside to draw the bead on
any one or each and praps even all? You
think love's got it in itself to perp the
panic that slams every single window cept
the one that lets it in? Or could it be the
very key that peels the roof about itself to
86 your meshuga mirage of a matrix?

Don't gavel my buttocks, buster: not hardly
world enough for that. You're wallowing hard
amid the weightless paraphernalia: no order
to be called to today, today. That thing that
gives the murky muddle a shape that can be
*read* has got to be the verysame you'd keep
tame in the box where you trap the fireflies.

Release it. Feed it. Give it a leg up. Got to
call it love. Not of all the crazed caboodle:
God's bizness, not ours. No, leave the
everything everywhere and cherish that
single set of eyes: accept a solace fiercely
solitary and watch the flowers erupt on Io.

## Mowing

Alan hates the trees. He mows the lawn in
brutal detail but tells me the trees have to
go. A legpull of course, but delivered with
such sweatfaced sincerity as to make me
wonder: what use are they, anyway? What's
their gig but the slopping of shade where
no one asked for it? Why redesign a garden
that was meant for sun some decade ago just
because the young maple we then decided
to tolerate has since inflated and reared itself
up and over the aster like some monstrous
marmot? Alan may have a point. Even
the trees we invited in—the row of pines
at the lower end—don't they jab monstrous
rips in the firmamental flow? Sprouting
higgledy-piggledy, defying form? And who
but Alan is our condottierre in the roughhouse
struggle to hang onto some approximation
of that very phantasm, form? Flowers too
are questionable unless well out of the way,
and those quirky Berkshire thunderstorms
crashing through the valleys with the express
intention of disrupting a working man's
hardset schedule: they also could be done
without. Life's far too hard for bolts from
the blue, says Alan with a chuckle, and
done for now with bonhommie he clamps on
the earplugs and bends to the endless task.

★ ★ ★ ★

## Brouha at the Checkpoint

It's not so much that that
orchard where I pick your
oranges on the increasingly
rare occasions when your
fear of me is overcome by
your need for the kind of
labor your own people are
so much too good for and to
which raw need and an aching
heart drive me without the
slightest hesitation or slur of
reproach: not so much that
that orchard of yours was
onetime owned and assiduously
cultivated by my veryown
grandfather at the end of a
sweatfaced parade of careful
and largely quiet men emanating
from one we know bore both my
name and perhaps my crooked
pinkie as he paid his feudal
portion to King Guy of
Jerusalem until Mister
Saladin whipped the royal
ass and spared the royal neck.

No not so much that and hardly
at all your occidental contempt
for my loving cultivation of
each and every opportunity to
miss an opportunity—no not any
of that that gets my longgone
graw: it's more a matter of
patience versus turpitude of

achievement versus being of
(dare I say this) success versus
victory no not the victory you
and your Mizraim pals scrapped
for farside Sinai no I trill with
my womenfolk a triumph of
olive over terrible taste: of
warmth over calculation
and today over tomorrow.

Yesterday of course is quite
another matter but do we
never get to crumble the
memory into something less
precise than slaughter? There's
a sun there are freckles there are
irregularities in the bowels yet
something shoves us toward
a firming of finalities and
even exhaustion can prove a
reckless current: consider if
you can the texture of despair.

Thread into needle is still
pretty remarkable as is adzing
the door to fit the frame yes
small precision's a blessing:
only when it gets larger does
it sear the veins: I say we ask
too much when we ask the
herons by what calculation
they find their way back.

Raise the gate a smidgin:
give this breeze a little slack.

★ ★ ★ ★

## Jitterditty in Ab

*("Jitters at the White House,"*
*New York Times: October 14, 2005)*

dizzle dazzle dumpling
toes in a well
faces in the toppingpot
right where they fell

souls in the laundry bag
propped against the gate
strike a match to find the latch
and slide them to their fate

## Friendly's on Route 2

Colossal burger and supermelt
are two different worlds: one's
highwinged periphery carried to a
quantum the other a lesson in
mortality topped by a crabby
slab of Peergynt's onion,
the one that hasn't a heart.
Grass outside's greener than it
ought to be, traffic is spotty, the
fuzztopped lady in different
shades of blue discovers it's
time to cross the street and
as for me I settle for the melt.

## A Tooth Slated for Extraction Next Wednesday

Condemned but unrepentant it
fills its space with that same
dumb quiescence that had to
be its undoing. Never managed
the smartaleck gumption that
might well have served the
function of a longgone crown.
How now to relate? Things lost
but still in play do have their way
of redefining time. As when
calm Tom Costello stopped me
on the street to invite me to his
own wake just one month down
the calendar: he himself missed
it by less than a day, but wasn't
he already gone? Is he so now?
My tongue pokes and slithers
to check the inventory: will it
pull back baffled Thursday next
or just possibly find a way to
contain so vast a thing as
absence? A baron more a
baron less said Chekhov but
for now I take it as it comes.

## Audubon Sanctuary, Wellfleet

Beachgrass in swirls that deny all
direction: the green waves in waves,
the brown hardly at all and with the
grey the swirl's there to stay—jiggles
a bit but mainly locked into that
awful fragility of stability. Not a
lot of color but what there is is on
the attack, green ever the aggressor
swiping sunlight toward the unarmored
eye: shade subdues it but only in fits and
flickers. White's up there in squeeky
streaks sifting into kewtips puffed and
peppered along a rim that ought to have
some significance but blue's a toughie
and where's horizon at all when the
puffs themselves accept the dye? Back
fast: comfort's down here among separate
things that flap and crawl: grace hangs its
hat in messy places where flesh decays and
sap flows and twisted treelets flick those
flares from shuddering spearheads.

Strange bird rustles the foliage: an oriole
perhaps? Turtles try to be islands: odd.
That same drift that shifts all shape toward
something like sameness strains as well to
hold the margins apart: no exemption to grass
or tick or fiddlercrab or this exhausted heart.